SCHOLASTIC

Comprehension Skills

40 Short Passages for Close Reading

GRADE 1

New York • Toronto • London • Auckland • Sydney
Mexico City • New Delhi • Hong Kong • Buenos Aires

Teaching *Resources*

Cover design by Jorge J. Namerow
Interior design by Jason Robinson
Illustrations by Mike Gordon

ISBN: 978-0-545-46052-1
Text and illustrations copyright © 2012 by Scholastic Inc.
Published by Scholastic Inc.
All rights reserved.
Printed in the U.S.A.

1 2 3 4 5 6 7 8 9 10   40   19 18 17 16 15 14 13 12

Contents

Passages

Using This Book

Reading comprehension in nonfiction involves numerous thinking skills. Students require these skills to make sense of a text and become successful readers. This book offers practice in key skills needed to meet the Common Core State Standards in Reading/Language Arts for grade one. (See page 6 for more.) Each student page includes a short passage focusing on three of these essential comprehension skills.

Comprehension Skills At-a-Glance

Use the information that follows to introduce the reading comprehension skills covered in this book.

Main Idea & Details

Understanding the main or key idea of a paragraph is crucial for a reader. The main idea is what the paragraph is about. The other parts of the paragraph help to explain more about this key idea. Sometimes, the main idea is in the first sentence of a paragraph.

The information that supports the main idea is usually referred to as the details. Details help a reader gain a fuller understanding of a paragraph.

Sequence

Readers need to understand that when several things happen in a paragraph or a story, they occur in sequence. Following the sequence of a selection helps readers recognize the time order of events or the order in which steps are taken. Students should become aware of common words or phrases which signal sequence, such as *first, then, next,* and *finally.*

Context Clues

Using context means determining an unfamiliar word's meaning by studying the phrases, sentences, and overall text with which the word appears. Context clues help readers comprehend and enjoy a text and also read more smoothly and efficiently.

Compare & Contrast

Recognizing how events, characters, places, and facts are alike and different helps a reader gain a richer understanding of a text. Sometimes a reader can learn more about something by finding out what it is *not* like than what it is like. A comparison shows similarities, while a contrast shows differences.

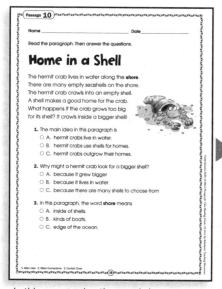

In "Plants We Eat," the first sentence identifies the main idea. The main idea is supported by examples in the rest of the paragraph.

In this paragraph, other words in the sentence provide a context for comprehending the word *shore.*

Predict

Good readers take time to think about a text. One way they do this is by thinking ahead to determine what may happen next or how an event will unfold. Often, information a reader has come across in the text provides clues to what will happen next. In many cases readers also use what they already know when they make predictions.

Inference

Although most primary students don't know what an inference is, many are most likely making inferences—both in their daily lives and when reading—without being aware of it. Students should understand that writers don't include every detail in their writing; it is up to readers to supply some information. A reader makes a guess or inference by putting together what is in a text with what he or she already knows. Inferring makes a significant difference in how much a reader gains from a text.

Make Connections

Good readers learn that there are connections between characters, events, ideas, or pieces of information in a text. Recognizing these relationships is an important way for readers to deepen their understanding of a text.

Fact & Opinion

Readers who can identify and differentiate between statements of fact and opinion are better able to analyze and assess a text. Students should learn to recognize phrases such as *I think* and *you should*, that signal opinions.

The writer never says what Petra and her father are doing, but information in the paragraph plus what readers already know helps make it clear.

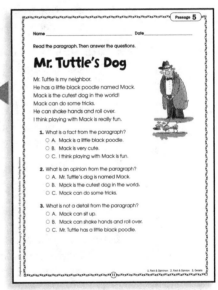

To appreciate this story, the reader should understand that the writer has shared several opinions as well as some facts about the neighbor's dog.

Tips

★ Tell students to first read the passage and then answer the questions. Show them how to fill in the circles for bubble-test questions.

★ The comprehension skills targeted in the questions accompanying each passage are labeled at the bottom of the page.

★ Review the completed pages with students on a regular basis. Encourage them to explain their thinking for each correct answer.

Meeting the Common Core State Standards

The passages and comprehension questions in this book are designed to help you meet both your specific English/Language Arts standards and learning expectations as well as those recommended by the Common Core State Standards Initiative (CCSSI). The activities in this book align with the following CCSSI standards for grade one.

Reading Standards for Literature

Key Ideas and Details
1. Ask and answer questions about key details in a text.
3. Describe characters, settings, and major events in a story, using key details.

Craft and Structure
4. Identify words and phrases in stories that suggest feelings or appeal to the senses.

Integration of Knowledge and Ideas
7. Use illustrations and details in a story to describe its characters, setting, or events.

Range of Reading and Level of Text Complexity
10. With prompting and support, read prose of appropriate complexity for grade 1.

Reading Standards for Informational Text

Key Ideas and Details
1. Ask and answer questions about key details in a text.
2. Identify the main topic and retell key details of a text.
3. Describe the connection between two individuals, events, ideas, or pieces of information in a text.

Craft and Structure
4. Ask and answer questions to help determine or clarify the meaning of words and phrases in a text.

Integration of Knowledge and Ideas
7. Use the illustrations and details in a text to describe its key ideas.
8. Identify the reasons an author gives to support points in a text.

Range of Reading and Level of Text Complexity
10. With prompting and support, read informational text appropriately complex for grade 1.

Reading Standards: Foundational Skills

Fluency
4. Read with sufficient accuracy and fluency to support comprehension.
   a. Read on-level text with purpose and understanding.
   c. Use context to confirm or self-correct word recognition and understanding, rereading as necessary.

Language Standards

Vocabulary Acquisition and Use
4. Determine or clarify the meaning of unknown and multiple-meaning words and phrases based on *grade 1 reading and content*, choosing flexibly from an array of strategies.
   a. Use sentence-level context as a clue to the meaning of a word or phrase.
5. With guidance and support from adults, demonstrate understanding of word relationships and nuances in word meanings.
   d. Distinguish shades of meaning among verbs differing in manner by defining or choosing them.
6. Use words and phrases acquired through conversations, reading and being read to, and responding to texts.

Name _____   Date _____

Read the paragraph. Then answer the questions.

The Robin's Nest

The robin wanted to build a nest.
First, she found some grass and straw.
Then she took the grass and straw to a tree.
Next, she put the grass and straw
together to make a nest.
Finally, she laid her eggs in the nest.

1. What did the robin do first?
   ○ A. She took the grass and straw to a tree.
   ○ B. She put the grass and straw together.
   ○ C. She found some grass and straw.

2. What did the robin do last?
   ○ A. She laid her eggs.
   ○ B. She found some grass and straw.
   ○ C. She looked for food.

3. In the story, the word **finally** means
   ○ A. first.
   ○ B. last.
   ○ C. next.

1. Sequence 2. Sequence 3. Context Clues

Name _____ Date_____

Read the paragraph. Then answer the questions.

You've Got Mail!

Suki got an e-mail from her friend, Annie.
The e-mail made Suki happy.
She went to talk to her mom.
Then she looked at the calendar.
Suki wrote back to Annie.
The answer was "Yes!"

1. Which sentence is most likely true?

○ A. Annie sent an e-mail to Suki's mom.

○ B. Annie asked about homework.

○ C. Suki made a date to see her friend.

2. What happened last?

○ A. Suki talked to her mom.

○ B. Suki got an e-mail.

○ C. Suki wrote back to her friend.

3. Why do you think Suki talked to her mom?

○ A. to find out what was for dinner

○ B. to ask if she could make a date with Annie

○ C. to ask for a snack

Name _____ Date_____

Read the paragraph. Then answer the questions.

The Nose Knows

When dogs meet, they sniff each other.
Dogs use their sense of smell to learn
about each other. Dogs can smell
many things that people cannot smell.
They **explore** the world with their noses.
They can learn a lot through their sense of smell.

1. The main idea of this paragraph is
   - ○ A. dogs do not have a good sense of smell.
   - ○ B. dogs use their sense of smell in different ways.
   - ○ C. dogs sniff each other.

2. A detail in this paragraph is
   - ○ A. people can smell things that dogs can't smell.
   - ○ B. dogs sniff each other when they meet.
   - ○ C. dogs cannot smell well.

3. In this paragraph, the word **explore** means
   - ○ A. run away.
   - ○ B. go on a trip.
   - ○ C. find out things.

1. Main Idea   2. Details   3. Context Clues

Name _____ Date _____

Read the paragraph. Then answer the questions.

Underground Town

Have you ever seen a prairie dog town?
That is where prairie dogs live.
But this town has no buildings or houses.
Prairie dogs live underground.
They dig deep into the earth
to make tunnels. Along the tunnels
are rooms for sleeping or storing food.
One room is lined with grass for the babies!

1. The main idea of this paragraph is
   - ○ A. towns without buildings.
   - ○ B. raising young prairie dogs.
   - ○ C. tunnel homes for prairie dogs.

2. A detail in the paragraph is
   - ○ A. underground town.
   - ○ B. where prairie dogs live.
   - ○ C. rooms for storing food.

3. You can guess that prairie dogs live
   - ○ A. alone.
   - ○ B. in pairs.
   - ○ C. in groups.

1. Main Idea 2. Details 3. Inference

Name _____ **Date** _____

Read the paragraph. Then answer the questions.

Mr. Tuttle's Dog

Mr. Tuttle is my neighbor.

He has a little black poodle named Mack.

Mack is the cutest dog in the world!

Mack can do some tricks.

He can shake hands and roll over.

I think playing with Mack is really fun.

1. What is a fact from the paragraph?
- ○ A. Mack is a little black poodle.
- ○ B. Mack is very cute.
- ○ C. I think playing with Mack is fun.

2. What is an opinion from the paragraph?
- ○ A. Mr. Tuttle's dog is named Mack.
- ○ B. Mack is the cutest dog in the world.
- ○ C. Mack can do some tricks.

3. What is not a detail from the paragraph?
- ○ A. Mack can sit up.
- ○ B. Mack can shake hands and roll over.
- ○ C. Mr. Tuttle has a little black poodle.

1. Fact & Opinion 2. Fact & Opinion 3. Details

Name _____ Date _____

Read the paragraph. Then answer the questions.

Snakes Are Everywhere!

Some snakes live in forests.
Some live in hot, dry deserts.
Others live in lakes or streams.
Some snakes even live in the sea!
Snakes live almost everywhere.
But they never live where
it is always freezing cold.

1. What is the main idea of this paragraph?

○ A. Snakes can live in trees.

○ B. Snakes live almost everywhere.

○ C. Snakes do not like freezing weather.

2. Which is a detail from the paragraph?

○ A. The author does not like snakes.

○ B. Some snakes live in the sea.

○ C. Snakes never go underground.

3. Snakes cannot live

○ A. where it is always very cold.

○ B. in forests.

○ C. in lakes or streams.

Name _____ **Date**_____

Read the paragraph. Then answer the questions.

Sally's Snack

Sally **dashed** from the elevator.
She gave her grandma a quick hug
at the door. She dropped her
book bag on the table.
Then Sally headed for the kitchen.
Out came the bread.
Out came the jam.
In no time, Sally made a snack.

1. Which sentence is most likely true?

○ A. Sally does not have any homework.

○ B. Sally likes peanut butter on bread.

○ C. Sally is hungry after school.

2. What did Sally have for a snack?

○ A. peanut butter on bread

○ B. cookies

○ C. jam on bread

3. The word **dashed** in this story means

○ A. ran in a hurry.

○ B. stopped.

○ C. a little bit.

1. Inference 2. Details 3. Context Clues

Name _____ Date _____

Read the paragraph. Then answer the questions.

Cool Penguins

Penguins live at the South Pole.
It is as far south as you can go.
It is one of the coldest places on Earth.
Penguins know how to live in the cold.
Their black and white feathers
form a warm coat. They also have
thick fat to keep them warm.

1. What is the main idea of this paragraph?
   - ○ A. Penguins know how to live at the South Pole.
   - ○ B. Penguins have a black and white coat.
   - ○ C. Thick fat keeps penguins warm.

2. Why do penguins need a warm coat of feathers?
   - ○ A. to fly
   - ○ B. to keep them warm in the cold
   - ○ C. to find a mate

2. In this paragraph, the word **thick** means
   - ○ A. the opposite of slippery.
   - ○ B. the opposite of thin.
   - ○ C. the opposite of big.

Name _____ **Date**_____

Read the paragraph. Then answer the questions.

Robot to the Rescue

Urbie is a new robot.
It has cameras that act as eyes.
Urbie may one day go into burning buildings.
Inside, Urbie will search for people
with its camera eyes.
It will let firefighters know
where the people are.
Then the firefighters can save the people.

1. The main idea of this paragraph is
   ○ A. a robot that likes fires.
   ○ B. a robot that finds people in fires.
   ○ C. a robot that takes pictures of fires.

2. A detail in this paragraph is
   ○ A. Urbie has cameras for eyes.
   ○ B. Urbie can climb.
   ○ C. Urbie will talk to firefighters.

3. In the title, the word **rescue** means
   ○ A. act.
   ○ B. know.
   ○ C. save.

1. Main Idea   2. Details   3. Context Clues

Name _____   Date _____

Read the paragraph. Then answer the questions.

Home in a Shell

The hermit crab lives in water along the **shore**.
There are many empty seashells on the shore.
The hermit crab crawls into an empty shell.
A shell makes a good home for the crab.
What happens if the crab grows too big
for its shell? It crawls inside a bigger shell!

1. The main idea in this paragraph is
   ○ A. hermit crabs live in water.
   ○ B. hermit crabs use shells for homes.
   ○ C. hermit crabs outgrow their homes.

2. Why might a hermit crab look for a bigger shell?
   ○ A. because it grew bigger
   ○ B. because it lives in water
   ○ C. because there are many shells to choose from

3. In this paragraph, the word **shore** means
   ○ A. inside of shells.
   ○ B. kinds of boats.
   ○ C. edge of the ocean.

Name _____ Date_____

Read the paragraph. Then answer the questions.

Snow!

Molly loves the snow.
As soon as the first **flakes** fall,
she gets out her sled.
She can't wait to slide down the hill.
Molly also loves to go skiing with her dad.
She likes making snow people and snow animals, too.
She even loves the way snow looks.

1. The main idea of this story is
   - ○ A. Molly loves to go skiing.
   - ○ B. Molly loves the snow.
   - ○ C. Molly likes to slide down the hill.

2. You can guess that Molly likes
   - ○ A. staying indoors.
   - ○ B. playing outdoors.
   - ○ C. summer days.

3. The word **flakes** in this story means
   - ○ A. cold cereal.
   - ○ B. little bits of snow.
   - ○ C. pretends.

1. Main Idea 2. Inference 3. Context Clues

Name _____ Date_____

Read the paragraph. Then answer the questions.

Polly Wants a Cracker?

Have you ever heard a parrot talk?
Parrots can copy sounds that they hear.
That is so cool! You can **train**
a parrot to repeat words and songs.
But a parrot cannot say words that
it has never heard. People can use
words to make new sentences.
A parrot cannot do this.

1. Which sentence is a fact?
   - ○ A. A parrot can make up a fairy tale.
   - ○ B. A parrot can copy sounds it hears.
   - ○ C. A parrot can answer any question.

2. Which sentence is an opinion?
   - ○ A. You can train a parrot to repeat words.
   - ○ B. A parrot can copy sounds it hears.
   - ○ C. That is so cool!

3. The word **train** in this paragraph means
   - ○ A. a long piece of cloth.
   - ○ B. teach.
   - ○ C. a group of railroad cars.

Name _____ Date_____

Read the paragraph. Then answer the questions.

The Biggest Spoon

What is the biggest spoon in the world?
It is a group of bright stars called the Big Dipper.
On a **clear** night, look up at the sky.
The Big Dipper might be right side up.
It might be upside down!
People can use the Big Dipper
to find their way when they get lost.

1. What is the main idea of this paragraph?
   ○ A. The Big Dipper is a group of stars.
   ○ B. You need a big spoon to eat.
   ○ C. The Big Dipper may be upside down.

2. You can guess that the Big Dipper is
   ○ A. hard to see in fog.
   ○ B. easy to see in the sun.
   ○ C. easy to see indoors.

3. In this paragraph, the word **clear** means
   ○ A. dark.
   ○ B. rainy.
   ○ C. not cloudy.

1. Main Idea 2. Inference 3. Context Clues

Name _____ Date _____

Read the paragraph. Then answer the questions.

The Costume Party

Kiki was invited to a costume party.
She wanted to go very much.
But, she did not know what to wear.
She asked her mom if she could buy a costume.
Her mom said it would cost too much.
Kiki looked through all the closets for ideas.
Then she **spotted** some boots and poles.

1. What happened first?
   ○ A. Kiki looked in the closets.
   ○ B. Kiki was invited to a party.
   ○ C. Kiki asked her mom to buy a costume.

2. What will Kiki most likely do?
   ○ A. Kiki will dress up as a skier.
   ○ B. Kiki will not go to the party.
   ○ C. Kiki will borrow a friend's costume.

3. In this story, the word **spotted** means
   ○ A. covered with dots.
   ○ B. saw.
   ○ C. took.

Name _____ Date _____

Read the paragraph. Then answer the questions.

Silly for Seuss

On March 2, kids put on silly hats.
They read silly books. Why?
It is Dr. Seuss's birthday! Dr. Seuss wrote
The Cat in the Hat, Green Eggs and Ham,
and many other books.
He drew most of the pictures, too.
How did he write such silly stories?
He put on funny hats to help him
get in a silly **mood**.

1. The main idea of this paragraph is
   - ○ A. silly hats for readers.
   - ○ B. Dr. Seuss's birthday.
   - ○ C. books by Dr. Seuss.

2. You can guess that kids
   - ○ A. like Dr. Seuss books.
   - ○ B. draw silly pictures.
   - ○ C. make funny hats.

3. The word **mood** in this paragraph means
   - ○ A. funny.
   - ○ B. the way a person feels.
   - ○ C. happy.

1. Main Idea   2. Inference   3. Context Clues

Name _____   Date_____

Read the paragraph. Then answer the questions.

The Secret Plan

Petra and her father had a secret plan.
They waited until Petra's mother went out.
Then they took out a bowl, a cake mix,
some eggs, and other things they needed.
They mixed and stirred. They put the batter
in the oven. Then they checked. Yes!
They had just enough birthday candles.

1. What do you think Petra and her father were doing?

- ○ A. making breakfast
- ○ B. cleaning up the kitchen
- ○ C. baking a birthday cake

2. How do you know it was a surprise?

- ○ A. They waited until the cake was done.
- ○ B. They waited to see if they had candles.
- ○ C. They waited until Petra's mother went out.

3. What did they do first?

- ○ A. They put the batter in the oven.
- ○ B. They took out the things they needed.
- ○ C. They mixed and stirred the batter.

1. Inference 2. Inference 3. Sequence

Name _____ Date_____

Read the paragraph. Then answer the questions.

About Owls

Did you know that owls have ears?
In fact, owls have large ears.
Their ears are good for listening
to night sounds. Owls also have
big eyes that see well in the dark.
Owls have big wings, too.
Their large wings do not **flap** loudly
when an owl flies after its dinner.

WHOO?

1. Their big ears, eyes, and wings
   - ○ A. hide owls.
   - ○ B. help owls.
   - ○ C. hurt owls.

2. Which sentence is most likely true?
   - ○ A. Owls are quiet when they hunt.
   - ○ B. Owls hunt in the daytime.
   - ○ C. Owls hunt for plants.

3. In this paragraph, the word **flap** means
   - ○ A. hit something.
   - ○ B. fall down.
   - ○ C. move up and down.

1. Make Connections 2. Inference 3. Context Clues

Name _____   Date_____

Read the paragraph. Then answer the questions.

Keeping Food Fresh

Long ago there were no freezers or cans.
How did people **preserve** (PREE-zerv) food—
keep it from going bad?
To keep meat fresh, they stored it in salt.
They hung up fruits and vegetables to dry them.
They put foods like carrots in cold places.
They also buried eggs in straw.
Then the foods stayed good for a long time.

1. The main idea of this paragraph is
   ○ A. ways people kept food from going bad.
   ○ B. kinds of food people ate.
   ○ C. how people buried eggs.

2. A detail in this paragraph is
   ○ A. people dried fruits and vegetables.
   ○ B. people used salt to keep eggs fresh.
   ○ C. people put meat in cold places.

3. In this paragraph, the word **preserve** means
   ○ A. do a job.
   ○ B. jam.
   ○ C. keep foods safe to eat.

Name _____ Date_____

Read the paragraph. Then answer the questions.

Summer Fun

It was a hot day. Evan was sitting
on the sand near the water.
Some people were swimming.
Evan picked up some wet sand.
He put it on the wall of his castle.
Then he packed it down.
The castle was looking good!
He picked up a shell.
"This could be a door," he thought.

1. Where does this story take place?
   - ○ A. in Evan's backyard
   - ○ B. at the beach
   - ○ C. in a sandbox

2. What is the main idea of this story?
   - ○ A. It was a hot summer day.
   - ○ B. Evan is making a sand castle.
   - ○ C. Evan was sitting on the sand.

3. What is an opinion in this story?
   - ○ A. Evan picked up some wet sand.
   - ○ B. Some people were swimming.
   - ○ C. The castle was looking good!

1. Inference 2. Main Idea 3. Fact & Opinion

Name _____ Date_____

Read the paragraph. Then answer the questions.

The Forgotten Panda

Each morning Gail walks Carol, her little sister,
to school. She holds her hand.
Gail makes sure Carol gets to her classroom.
Today Carol is crying. She is **upset**. Why?
Carol forgot her panda for show-and-tell.
Gail cannot get her sister to stop crying.

1. What will most likely happen next?

   ○ A. Gail will send Carol home to get the panda.

   ○ B. Gail will leave Carol on the sidewalk crying.

   ○ C. Gail will take Carol home to get the panda.

2. From this story you can guess that

   ○ A. Gail is a good sister.

   ○ B. Gail forgot Carol.

   ○ C. Gail forgot the panda.

3. The word **upset** in this story means

   ○ A. knock over.

   ○ B. unhappy.

   ○ C. upside down.

1. Predict   2. Inference   3. Context Clues

Name _____ Date _____

Read the paragraph. Then answer the questions.

Up in the Clouds

Look up at the clouds in the sky.
Do they look white and puffy?
Then it will be a sunny day.
Are the clouds thin? Do they look like
wisps of hair covering the sky?
That means it might rain.
Sometimes clouds are dark and piled up high.
That means a storm might be coming!

1. What is this paragraph mostly about?
- ○ A. clouds
- ○ B. thunderstorms
- ○ C. rainy weather

2. Another good title for this paragraph would be
- ○ A. Clouds Bring Snow.
- ○ B. Clouds and the Weather.
- ○ C. A Sky Without Clouds.

3. The word **sometimes** in this paragraph means
- ○ A. all the time.
- ○ B. now and then.
- ○ C. at no time.

Name _____ Date_____

Read the paragraph. Then answer the questions.

Meet Irv

Irv likes to try new things.

He likes to taste new foods.

He likes knowing how to do the latest dances.

Today Irv is trying to learn how to rollerblade.

His friends laugh at his **wobbly** steps.

But that doesn't bother him.

Oops! Irv just tripped and fell.

1. What will most likely happen next?

○ A. Irv will give up and go home.

○ B. Irv will get up and try again.

○ C. Irv will hide from his friends.

2. What happens first?

○ A. Irv trips.

○ B. Irv's friends laugh.

○ C. Irv tries to rollerblade.

3. The word **wobbly** in this paragraph means

○ A. silly.

○ B. fancy.

○ C. unsteady.

Name _____ **Date** _____

Read the paragraph. Then answer the questions.

Clever Cat

Pepper the cat saved his house from a fire.
How? When a fire started, Pepper didn't **panic**.
He unlocked a window with his paw.
Then he went out the window.
People saw smoke coming out of the window.
Firefighters came and put out the fire.
Pepper saved the day!

1. The main idea of this paragraph is
   - ○ A. how Pepper opened a window.
   - ○ B. how Pepper saved his house.
   - ○ C. how Pepper put out a fire.

2. How did the firefighters most likely know about the fire?
   - ○ A. Pepper told them.
   - ○ B. People saw smoke and called them.
   - ○ C. The house owners told them.

3. The word **panic** in this paragraph means
   - ○ A. get burned.
   - ○ B. something to cook in.
   - ○ C. get very scared.

1. Main Idea 2. Inference 3. Context Clues

Name _____ Date _____

Read the paragraph. Then answer the questions.

Plants We Eat

We eat many foods that come from plants.
Do you eat apples and bananas?
They are fruits. Do you eat toast or cereal?
They are made from grains like wheat,
oats, and rice. How about carrots,
celery, and potatoes? They are vegetables.
Fruits, grains, and vegetables all come from plants.

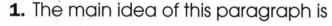

1. The main idea of this paragraph is
   - ○ A. cereal is made from grains.
   - ○ B. carrots are vegetables.
   - ○ C. many foods we eat come from plants.

2. Apples are
   - ○ A. vegetables.
   - ○ B. fruits.
   - ○ C. grains.

3. If you eat a banana on cereal, you eat
   - ○ A. fruit and grains.
   - ○ B. two vegetables.
   - ○ C. plants and animals.

1. Main Idea   2. Details   3. Make Connections

Name _____ Date_____

Read the paragraph. Then answer the questions.

My Monster

I saw a scary monster who lived in a cave.
He had shaggy fur and a long, striped tail.
He had big, **pointy** teeth.
His three horns looked like arrows.
One of his feet was bigger than the other three.
"Wake up! Time for breakfast," called Mom.
Oh, good! It was only a dream.

1. How many feet did the monster have?

○ A. two

○ B. four

○ C. three

2. You can tell that the child in this story

○ A. was late for breakfast.

○ B. liked monsters.

○ C. had a nightmare.

3. The word **pointy** in this story means

○ A. with a sharp tip.

○ B. striped.

○ C. round.

1. Make Connections 2. Inference 3. Context Clues

Name _____ **Date** __

Read the paragraph. Then answer the questions.

Storm in the Night

CRASH! Thunder woke Tim up!
A few drops of rain hit the windowsill.
A flash of lightning lit up the sky.
Tim counted, "One . . . two . . . three . . .
four . . . five." Then thunder boomed again,
even louder than before. "Five seconds," said Tim.
"That means the storm is about one mile away."

1. Tim woke up because he
   - ○ A. got wet from the rain.
   - ○ B. wanted to see the storm.
   - ○ C. heard thunder.

2. Why did Tim count to five?
   - ○ A. He was scared.
   - ○ B. He could not hear the thunder.
   - ○ C. He wanted to find out how close the storm was.

3. In this paragraph, the word **crash** means
   - ○ A. sudden, loud noise.
   - ○ B. rainfall.
   - ○ C. accident.

1. Details 2. Inference 3. Context Clues

Name _____ Date_____

Read the paragraph. Then answer the questions.

What's on Mars?

The planet Mars is called the Red Planet.
That's because it is covered in reddish dust.
How did scientists learn what Mars is like?
They sent a robot to Mars.
The robot collected rocks and dirt.
It also took pictures and sent them back to Earth.
Scientists studied the rocks, dirt, and pictures.
They learned that Mars is cold and **dry**.

1. What did the robot do after it took pictures?
- ○ A. It collected rocks.
- ○ B. It sent them to Earth.
- ○ C. It landed on Mars.

2. The pictures must have showed that Mars is
- ○ A. hot.
- ○ B. wet.
- ○ C. red.

3. The word **dry** in this paragraph means
- ○ A. dirty.
- ○ B. not wet.
- ○ C. rocky.

Name _____ Date_____

Read the paragraph. Then answer the questions.

High Waters

What causes floods? Floods happen
most often in the spring. Snow melts
off the mountains and turns to water.
The water runs down into rivers.
Rainstorms may add even more water to the rivers.
The water rises and overflows the riverbanks.
These high waters can flood fields and towns.

1. You can predict that a lot of snow in winter can
- ○ A. cause floods.
- ○ B. cause rainstorms.
- ○ C. cause low rivers.

2. When are floods most likely to happen?
- ○ A. in summer
- ○ B. in winter
- ○ C. in spring

3. You can guess that snow melts when
- ○ A. it gets cold.
- ○ B. it gets warm.
- ○ C. rivers overflow.

1. Predict   2. Details   3. Inference

Name _____ Date _____

Read the paragraph. Then answer the questions.

Queen of the Dinosaurs

Who is the "Queen of the Dinosaurs"?
It is Sue, the biggest T. rex dinosaur ever found.
Sue was a meat-eating dinosaur.
Her head **alone** was five feet long.
One of her teeth was more than a foot long!
Sue's bones were buried for millions of years.
Over time, they became hard as stone
and turned into fossils.

1. Why is Sue called "Queen of the Dinosaurs"?
   ○ A. She ruled over the other dinosaurs.
   ○ B. She is the biggest dinosaur ever found.
   ○ C. She was a good hunter.

2. How do you know that Sue lived a long time ago?
   ○ A. She ate meat.
   ○ B. Her head was five feet long.
   ○ C. Her bones were buried for millions of years.

3. The word **alone** in the paragraph means
   ○ A. by itself.
   ○ B. alike.
   ○ C. in the earth.

1. Main Idea   2. Make Connections   3. Context Clues

Name _____ Date _____

Read the paragraph. Then answer the questions.

What's Going On?

Tyler found red spots on his face and arms.
He scratched until his mom came to take him home.
A week later, Jin and Yanna got spots, too.
The next Monday, six more children
were absent. Finally, everyone got well
and came back to school.
But this time, the teacher was absent.
Guess what was wrong with her!

1. What do you think was wrong with the children?
   - A. They had sore throats.
   - B. They had chickenpox.
   - C. They had broken arms.

2. How do you know the spots were itchy?
   - A. Jin said, "These spots itch!"
   - B. The teacher said so.
   - C. Tyler scratched them.

3. How many children in all got sick?
   - A. 5
   - B. 6
   - C. 9

Name _____ Date_____

Read the paragraph. Then answer the questions.

Life in the Ocean

The dolphin lives in the wide, open sea.
It **roams** the ocean to catch fish.
The dolphin does not swim too deep.
It must come up to breathe.
The anglerfish lives in the deep, dark sea.
It makes its own light with a light pole on its head!
What happens when other fish swim toward the light?
The anglerfish catches them.

1. How are a dolphin and an anglerfish alike?
   ○ A. They both live in the sea.
   ○ B. They both have a light pole.
   ○ C. They both need to breathe air.

2. How are an anglerfish and a dolphin different?
   ○ A. An anglerfish eats fish.
   ○ B. An anglerfish lives in the deep sea.
   ○ C. A dolphin can swim.

3. In this paragraph, the word **roams** means
   ○ A. parts of a home.
   ○ B. looks for.
   ○ C. moves from place to place.

Name _____ Date _____

Read the paragraph. Then answer the questions.

Lunch Buddies

Roger was feeling a little sad.
It was the first day of school,
and he had no one to eat lunch with.
Roger saw a new boy who looked sad, too.
"Is something wrong?" Roger asked.
"I forgot to bring lunch money," said the boy.
"I have a big lunch," said Roger.
"Why don't you sit with me?
Then we can share."

1. This story is mostly about
   - ○ A. forgetting lunch.
   - ○ B. finding a lunch buddy.
   - ○ C. feeling hungry.

2. Where does this story take place?
   - ○ A. at Roger's home
   - ○ B. at school
   - ○ C. on the playground

3. What do you think will happen the next day?
   - ○ A. The new boy will forget his money.
   - ○ B. The boys will sit together.
   - ○ C. The boys will both feel sad.

Name _____ Date_____

Read the paragraph. Then answer the questions.

Ostriches

The ostrich is the biggest bird in the world.
An ostrich may grow as tall as eight feet.
It has strong legs and can run fast.
It is much too heavy to fly, though.
An ostrich can weigh as much as 345 pounds.
It lays the biggest eggs, too.
Just one ostrich egg can weigh three pounds!

1. The main idea of this paragraph is

    ○ A. an ostrich can grow as tall as eight feet.

    ○ B. an ostrich has strong legs.

    ○ C. the ostrich is the world's biggest bird.

2. What is a detail from the paragraph?

    ○ A. Ostriches lay the biggest eggs.

    ○ B. Ostriches eat plants and roots.

    ○ C. Ostriches fly well.

3. You can guess that an ostrich egg would be

    ○ A. a lot to eat for breakfast.

    ○ B. not much to eat for breakfast.

    ○ C. very bad to eat for breakfast.

1. Main Idea   2. Details   3. Inference

Name _____ Date _____

Read the paragraph. Then answer the questions.

Autumn Changes

The **season** after summer is autumn.
Autumn brings lots of changes.
The biggest change is the weather.
In some places it starts to get colder.
The cold makes leaves change color.
They change from green to red, orange, or yellow.
Then the leaves fall from the trees.
Maybe that is why autumn is sometimes called fall!

1. The main idea of this paragraph is that autumn brings
   ○ A. Halloween.
   ○ B. many changes.
   ○ C. leaves.

2. One detail about autumn is
   ○ A. the weather gets warmer.
   ○ B. leaves change color.
   ○ C. the days get longer.

3. In this paragraph, the word **season** means
   ○ A. part of the year.
   ○ B. salt and pepper.
   ○ C. time for school.

Name _____ **Date** _____

Read the paragraph. Then answer the questions.

Ice Hotel

Have you ever heard of a hotel
made of ice?
The Ice Hotel is in Sweden.
It gets very cold there in the winter.
The hotel is made of snow and ice.
Even the beds are made of ice.
The people who stay there sleep
in special, warm sleeping bags.
Every spring the Ice Hotel melts.
But in the fall, people build a new one!

1. The main idea of this paragraph is
   ○ A. hotels in Sweden.
   ○ B. winter in Sweden.
   ○ C. a hotel of ice and snow.

2. At the Ice Hotel, what do people sleep in to stay warm?
   ○ A. ice beds
   ○ B. sleeping bags
   ○ C. snow banks

3. Why do you think the Ice Hotel melts each spring?

_____

_____

1. Main Idea   2. Details   3. Inference

Name _____ Date_____

Read the paragraph. Then answer the questions.

Bats and Birds

Both bats and birds can fly.

You might see them on a rooftop.

In other ways, bats and birds are very different.

Birds have feathers. Bats have fur.

Birds have beaks. Bats have teeth.

Bats hang upside-down when they rest.

Birds never do that!

Bats and birds are very easy to tell apart

when they are not flying.

1. How are bats and birds alike?

○ A. Both have feathers.

○ B. Both hang upside-down.

○ C. Both can fly.

2. How are bats and birds different?

○ A. Bats land on rooftops.

○ B. Birds have teeth.

○ C. Bats have fur.

3. Write another way that bats and birds are different.

_____

_____

Name _____ Date_____

Read the paragraph. Then answer the questions.

Rachel's Recipe

On Saturday, Rachel got up early.
Her mom was still asleep,
so Rachel made her own breakfast.
She put some peanut butter in a bowl.
She mixed it with a little honey.
Then she stirred in some oatmeal,
bran flakes, and raisins. Rachel tried some.
It tasted yummy! When Mom got up, she said,
"Oh, good, you made granola!"

1. What did Rachel do on Saturday?
   - ○ A. She woke up Mom.
   - ○ B. She slept late.
   - ○ C. She made granola.

2. What word in the story tells how Mom felt?
   - ○ A. good
   - ○ B. sweet
   - ○ C. yummy

3. Which sentence is an opinion?
   - ○ A. Rachel made her own breakfast.
   - ○ B. She stirred in some oatmeal.
   - ○ C. It tasted yummy!

1. Main Idea 2. Details 3. Fact and Opinion

Name _____ Date _____

Read the paragraph. Then answer the questions.

Class Trip

Brian's class went on a trip.

It was a sunny spring day.

They took the bus to Pine Tree Farm.

At the farm, they saw chickens, pigs, and goats.

They watched someone milking cows.

There was a big vegetable garden, too.

The class helped pick peas and **spinach**.

It was a great way to learn about life on a farm!

1. The main idea of this story is

   ○ A. Brian's class saw many animals.

   ○ B. Brian's class went on a trip to a farm.

   ○ C. Brian's class helped pick peas.

2. A detail from this paragraph is

   ○ A. they milked cows.

   ○ B. they saw chickens, pigs, and goats.

   ○ C. they ate vegetables.

3. In this story, **spinach** is a kind of

   ○ A. vegetable.

   ○ B. animal.

   ○ C. garden.

Name _____ Date_____

Read the paragraph. Then answer the questions.

Scooters and Bikes

Scooters and bikes are fun to ride.
Scooters and most bikes have two wheels.
A scooter has no seat.
You ride it standing up.
You push on the ground
with one foot to start moving.
Then you **coast** with both feet on the scooter.
A bike has a seat and pedals.
You sit on the seat and push the pedals with your feet.
The wheels turn, and away you go!

1. How is a bike like a scooter?

○ A. Your feet push the pedals.

○ B. You can ride on it.

○ C. It has a seat.

2. How is a scooter different from a bike?

○ A. It is fun to ride.

○ B. It does not have a seat.

○ C. It has two wheels.

3. In the paragraph, the word **coast** means

○ A. seashore.

○ B. ride easily.

○ C. jacket.

1. Compare & Contrast 2. Compare & Contrast 3. Context Clues

Name _____ Date_____

Read the paragraph. Then answer the questions.

Chirp! Chirp! Chirp!

On warm summer nights, male crickets chirp.
They make short, sharp sounds.
Crickets do not use their mouths to chirp.
Instead, they rub their wings together.
Male crickets chirp to call female crickets.
The females hear the sounds and come closer.
After the crickets mate, the female lays eggs.
Soon there will be more chirping crickets!

1. Which sentence is a fact?
   - ○ A. A cricket's chirp is a nice sound.
   - ○ B. Baby crickets are cute.
   - ○ C. A cricket rubs its wings to chirp.

2. Which sentence is an opinion?
   - ○ A. Crickets chirp in the summer.
   - ○ B. Crickets make funny sounds.
   - ○ C. Female crickets lay eggs.

3. What happens first?
   - ○ A. Crickets mate.
   - ○ B. Females come close.
   - ○ C. Male crickets chirp.

Answers

page 7:
1. C
2. A
3. B

page 8:
1. C
2. C
3. B

page 9:
1. B
2. B
3. C

page 10:
1. C
2. C
3. C

page 11:
1. A
2. B
3. A

page 12:
1. B
2. B
3. A

page 13:
1. C
2. C
3. A

page 14:
1. A
2. B
3. B

page 15:
1. B
2. A
3. C

page 16:
1. B
2. A
3. C

page 17:
1. B
2. B
3. B

page 18:
1. B
2. C
3. B

page 19:
1. A
2. A
3. C

page 20:
1. B
2. A
3. B

page 21:
1. B
2. A
3. B

page 22:
1. C
2. C
3. B

page 23:
1. B
2. A
3. C

page 24:
1. A
2. A
3. C

page 25:
1. B
2. B
3. C

page 26:
1. C
2. A
3. B

page 27:
1. A
2. B
3. B

page 28:
1. B
2. C
3. C

page 29:
1. B
2. B
3. C

page 30:
1. C
2. B
3. A

page 31:
1. B
2. C
3. A

page 32:
1. C
2. C
3. A

page 33:
1. B
2. C
3. B

page 34:
1. A
2. C
3. B

page 35:
1. B
2. C
3. A

page 36:
1. B
2. C
3. C

page 37:
1. A
2. B
3. C

page 38:
1. B
2. B
3. B

page 39:
1. C
2. A
3. A

page 40:
1. B
2. B
3. A

page 41:
1. C
2. B
3. Possible: The weather gets warmer.

page 42:
1. C
2. C
3. Answers will vary but should reflect the text.

page 43:
1. C
2. A
3. C

page 44:
1. B
2. B
3. A

page 45:
1. B
2. B
3. B

page 46:
1. C
2. B
3. C